Seas & Skies

CÔTES-D'ARMOR

Philip Plisson ⚓ *Text by Dominique Le Brun*

Stewart, Tabori & Chang
New York

Whether writing about the sea, painting or photographing it, one thing is true – without a real affinity for the subject in hand, the artist or writer's talent alone will not suffice to convey the emotion that gives a photograph, a painting or a text all of its power. Yet this affinity with the sea is a mysterious thing. Where does it come from? Undoubtedly one should be a sailor, but that is not enough. The most important thing is the ability always to find the point of view that best illustrates the particularity of a maritime location or the best moment. The source of Philip Plisson's considerable talent lies in a respect for this approach that borders on the obsessive.

In perusing these collected pictures that illustrate the coast of the Côtes-d'Armor, I was astounded to see many places that are extremely tricky to navigate as a sailor, depicted with the eye of someone who clearly has experience of these waters from having diced with disaster there on more than one occasion. If I had to pick a word to describe the photographs presented in this book, then I would pick the word "truth". The coast of the Côtes-d'Armor is particularly

difficult to depict since it is forever changing according to the direction of the wind and the ebb and flow of the tides. Yet for each place there is an ideal meteorological situation and particular state of the sea that best expresses its character. Philip Plisson excels at capturing these moments so well that I suspect him of directing the tides and the winds as one would a model.

If there is one coast of France that can boast of having true character, then it is this northern coast of Brittany. What makes it truly exceptional is the variety of landscapes crossed as one travels down the Côtes-d'Armor. Of course the best thing is to take a sailing trip along the coast. One day you cast anchor in the shelter of an island such as Bréhat, Hébihens or Costaérès. The next day you moor at the quay of a mediaeval town at the top of an estuary, such as Lannion, Tréguier or Dinan. Then set sail the following morning for a deserted creek hidden away in a maze of islets, off Port-Blanc or Trégastel perhaps.

But you don't have to set foot on a boat to discover the best aspects of the Côtes-d'Armor coast. Firstly, because the Sentier du Littoral (coastal path) allows you to walk right along the edge of the coast from one end of the Côtes-d'Armor to the

other, a fabulous excursion! Secondly, during the periods of low tide you can wander out onto the foreshore, an enchanting kingdom of algae, sand and shells. The effects of the tides are particularly impressive on this coast, infinitely remoulding the landscape. During spring tides when the sea is out in the bays of Saint-Brieuc and La Fresnaye, the Channel seems to retreat beyond the horizon. And then there is the range of panoramic views made so much more magnificent by the climate, with its prevailing winds from the west that shift regularly from northwest to southwest, providing ever-changing and impressive skies.

It is impossible to claim to truly know the Côtes-d'Armor as long as one has not seen it at different levels of tide and in all weather conditions. Frankly, a lifetime would hardly suffice. But you may consider this little collection of photographs as an ideal way to view this coast under its best light. As sailors say: "Good sailing!"

Dominique Le Brun

Pages 6-7
The sands of Lieue-de-Grève stretch across
the innermost part of the bay of Lannion. A little way
out from the spur of rock embraced by
the waves, the sea laps around a large stone cross that
once served as a landmark to travellers taking
a shortcut across the bay at low tide.
It can still be seen today.

Pages 8-9
Yaudet Chapel overlooks the mouth of
the river Lannion; a number of thanksgiving plaques
are a reminder of how tricky navigation can be
on the coast of the Côtes-d'Armor.

Sailors can approach the estuary at night, guided by
the coloured panels of the Beg-Léguer lighthouse.

How calm it is in the Yaudet anchorage! The Servel
and Dourven points form a chicane that breaks
the very often heavy swell in the bay of Lannion.

The Trébeurden marina lies in the shelter of the island of Miliau: the boats are kept afloat at low tide by a moveable-sill system.

Although Île Grande lies just a few metres off the continent, its insular nature is hardly noticeable. Here we see Pors Gélin beach on the island's northern side.

The solitary Triagoz lighthouse stands fast amid the waves five nautical miles out from the north-west of Trégastel and so is known only to sailors. The architecture is quite impressive for a structure that cannot be seen from the coast!

Between Île Grande
and Trégastel,
a maze of rocks
and reefs guard
the anchorages
of Pors Gélin,
Toul-Bihan,
Coz-Porz
and others.
This apparently
intrepid fisherman
is one of the few
who know how
to weave their way
through the hazards
and out into
the open sea.

Pages 18-19
Here at Trégastel,
near the isle of Renote,
a myriad of large pink-granite
rocks, many of which are shaped
like animals, take on eerie
colours under early-morning
light or at dusk.

The islands of Cerfs, Rats,
Plate, Moines, Bono, Malban
and Rouzic run west to east
off the coast of Ploumanac'h
and make up the archipelago
of the Sept-Îles.
The islands provide nesting sites
for a number of birds threatened
with extinction and so have
the status of a nature reserve;
landing is permitted only on
the island of Moines.

One of the last non-automated lighthouses in France stands on the island of Moines. In the absence of fancy electronics, a keeper tends to the delicate operation of switching on the light and keeping watch.

Pages 24-25
A lighthouse guards Mean Ruz point near Ploumanac'h;
its tower was built from the same pink-granite stone as the rocks
that lie around it. As evening fades, the clouds floating over
the Sept-Îles seem to reflect the pink hues below.

The lifeboat is launched from a slipway at a point where
the water is always deep, even at low tide.

A string of coloured buoys mark the route through the thousands of rocks that guard Ploumanac'h port.

An elegant little dinghy finds a snug berth between two rocks.

29

The channel leading into Ploumanac'h port has been clearly marked out by the Department of Lighthouses and Beacons.

Beside the channel lies the islet of Costaérès and its castle built around 1900. One erstwhile guest was the novelist Henryk Sienkiewicz (Nobel Prize for Literature in 1905); perhaps the dramatic setting inspired his writing of The Teutonic Knights?

The exotic silhouettes of these palm trees are a reminder that the coast of Brittany enjoys a microclimate. Sheltered by Ploumanac'h point, Perros-Guirrec became a fashionable resort during the Belle Époque.

One day they will sail out to the islands on the horizon, but for now these kids practise their tacking aboard Optimist dinghies.

Pages 34-35
Perros-Guirrec was one
of the first artificial marinas
in Brittany, with a retaining
wall ensuring that the boats
stay afloat in the basin.

The archipelago that
stretches out before
Port-Blanc is truly a strange
landscape, for the islands
are linked together by pebble
paths which emerge at low
tide. The villas that were
constructed by the islands'
original rich owners are now
highly sought after by
those seeking solitude.

The houses in Port-Blanc are built on the very edge of the beach, sometimes even right against the rocks! The slipway is lined with prams, punts and other vessels which are used to reach the boats anchored in the shelter of the islands.

This small house built at the end of a dyke,
on one of the Port-Blanc islands, is a former tide-mill.
The incoming tide fills a basin, which empties
with the outgoing tide via a reach equipped
with a paddle wheel.

On the foreshore at Buguélès it is not always
easy to determine where the land ends
and the sea begins.

Pages 42-43
The little house built between two rocks is now known
all over the world! This emblem of the Côtes-d'Armor coast
stands at Plougrescant, near the Castel Meur rock.

Despite lying some way inland at the top of an estuary,
the mediaeval town of Tréguier – one of the seven
Breton bishoprics – is also a port.

The Roches Douvres lighthouse stands far from the Breton coast, practically halfway between Paimpol and the island of Guernsey.

The lighthouse's power-plant resembles a small factory, supplied with electricity by two wind turbines.

One of nature's more fantastic creations is the furrow of Talbert,
a stretch of sand and pebbles formed by tidal currents; it lies in
the west of the Bréhat archipelago and is over three miles long.

Farmers gather kelp and leave it in small clumps
to dry, before spreading it on their fields where it makes
an excellent natural fertiliser.

The Tourelle de la Vieille stands in front of the fishing port of Loguivy and marks the entry into the Trieux estuary, of which the Croix lighthouse and red Vincre tower are the main seamarks.

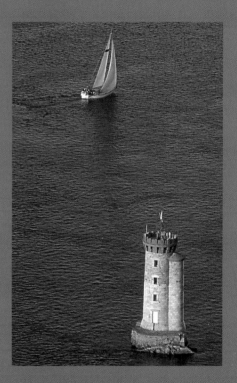

Boats tacking up the Trieux can tell how well
they are catching the wind and beating
the current by checking their position
in relation to the Croix lighthouse!

Pages 52-53
These two photographs depict the same location (the Bodic oyster-beds on the Trieux river) at low tide and at high tide. On this particular day the sea level varied in height by the equivalent of a two-storey building in just six hours!

The Bodic seamark-light stands in line with the Croix lighthouse and indicates the entry to the Trieux estuary at the island of Bréhat; sailors who stray from the proper line in these waters generally end up running aground.

Travel up the Trieux river until the old fortified town
of Pontrieux and as you come round the bend of a meander
you will suddenly stumble upon the chateau of la Roche-Jagu.
Don't worry, you're not dreaming! The chateau was built
by Catherine de Tronguindy in the 15th century;
today it houses exhibitions and hosts various cultural events.

On the islet of Roc'h ar On one can still see a former customs house
to which, so it is said, intemperate civil servants were posted to!

With its 187-foot high tower, Héaux-de-Bréhat is one
of the most majestic lighthouses on the French coast.
Its light can be seen for 15 nautical miles.

A bird's eye view of Loguivy-de-la-Mer.
Though small, this busy port specialises in catching shellfish.

*High tide over
the Bréhat
archipelago.
Most visitors
do not realise
that there are
a dozen islets
scattered round
the main island
– itself composed
of two pieces
of land separated
by an isthmus
a few metres wide
and spanned by
a little bridge!*

In the foreground of the aerial photograph one can see
the Birlot tide-mill; the port of la Corderie is in the centre;
behind it we see the northern part of the island
and the Paon lighthouse.

It is very hard to say who is the sovereign of Bréhat — the land
or the sea? A gate at the bottom of the garden opens onto
a mooring that is more than convenient at high tide!

*The
morning
mists
announce
another
glorious day
over Bréhat.*

At the extreme northern end of the island,
the Paon lighthouse seems to sit in the grasp
of a pink-granite hand. At high tide,
the waves crash down
around its long terrace.

Overlooking the Birlot tide-mill, the chapel of Saint-Michel
is painted white so as to serve as a seamark to sailors
approaching Bréhat from the north-west.

Opposite Porz-Éven, the island of Saint-Rion
has a number of plots of land used for organic farming.
In the background we can see Arcouest point
and the Bréhat archipelago.

The multitude of rocks and shallows swept by strong tidal currents
provide rich pickings for the many fishing boats that ply these waters.

Standing ten miles off the coast at the opening of the bay of
Saint-Brieuc, the bright red and white striped
Grand Léjon lighthouse is known only to those sailors
who have crossed from Cap Fréhel to the island of Bréhat.

The Lost-Pic lighthouse sits on its own little islet just out from
the cliffs; it indicates the easternmost end of the Paimpol cove.
For navigators, this is where the bay of Saint-Brieuc begins.

Accessible only at high tide via a lock that keeps the basins full
of water, Paimpol port is now devoted entirely to pleasure boats.
Up until the 1930s it was home to a flotilla of schooners
that left each year to fish for cod off the Icelandic coast.

Inside Paimpol church stands the statue
of Notre-Dame-de-Bonne-Nouvelle
(Our Lady of Good News), which was carried
in procession by the fishermen before they left for Iceland.

The ruins of Beauport on the edge of Paimpol cove have lost nothing of their majesty. This powerful abbey was erected in the 13th century and held sway over the whole region; so great was its wealth and influence that it was swiftly dismantled at the start of the French Revolution.

The eastern part
of the bay
of Saint-Brieuc,
between the
Gouessant estuary
and Val-André,
is occupied entirely
by the baskets
of the mussel beds.
The tide goes out
a long way, making
work much easier
and facilitating
the circulation
of tractors.

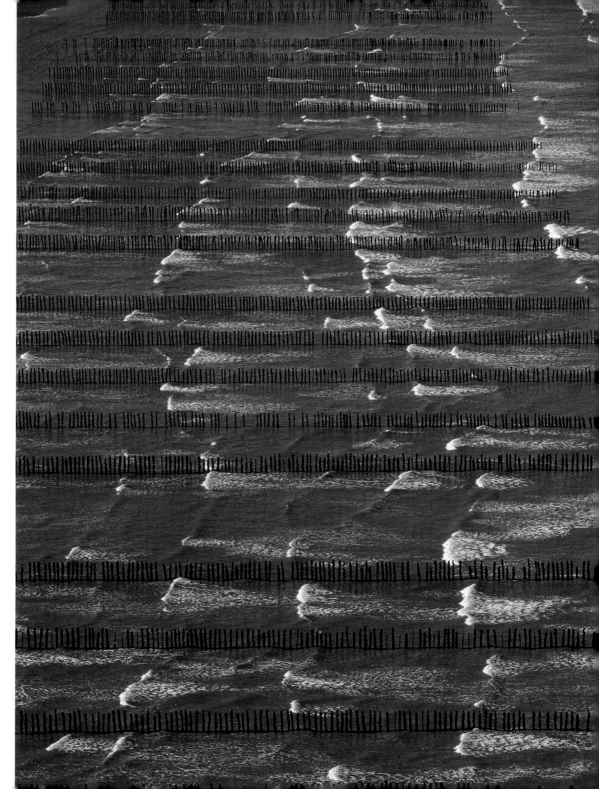

When the tide starts to come in, the mussel farmers quickly leave the beds for dry land on board their tractors. Soon, the waves are washing over the baskets, renewing the plankton and oxygenating the water.

The port of Erquy is home to a flotilla of coastal fishing boats. In winter they join their colleagues from Saint-Quay-Portrieux and dredge for scallops. But like many Breton ports, Erquy dries up at low tide.

The ports of the Côtes-d'Armor have remained
particularly attached to their maritime culture.
Erquy happily welcomes sailboats of old such
as the cutter Sainte-Jeanne *(main picture)*
or the Pauline, *a traditional Channel fishing boat.*

The islet of Saint-Michel Devant lies opposite the resort of Sables-d'Or-les-Pins, but is accessible at high tide only. Its little chapel is surmounted by a daring archangel who defies every storm!

Fort-la-Latte was built
at the opening of the
bay of La Fresnaye
to dissuade an English
fleet from anchoring
here while awaiting
the most favourable
circumstances to attack
Saint-Malo. Behind it
we see the Sévignés
cove and Cap Fréhel
with its lighthouse.

Cap Fréhel is one of the waypoints in the Route du Rhum race; every four years, a huge crowd gathers here to watch the competitors sail past.

The Cap Fréhel lighthouse was built in 1948, replacing an old 17ᵗʰ century tower that was destroyed during the Second World War.

Pages 88-89
This view of the anchorage
of Saint-Cast is typical
of traditional pleasure boating
in northern Brittany,
where little sailing boats
and motor cruisers lie stranded
on the silt at low tide.

The island of Hébihens
lies opposite Saint-Jacut
and makes a most welcoming
anchorage, since one or other
of its beaches is always
sheltered whatever the direction
of the wind. The tower that
overlooks the island supports
a platform on which a fire
used to be lit, so serving
as a makeshift lighthouse.

Between the port of Dinan and the village of Léhon, the Rance meanders between steep banks. The old towpath on its right bank is a favourite walk for many Dinan inhabitants.

After Dinan, the Rance river flows into the Ille-et-Rance Canal; this leads to Rennes where it joins the Vilaine river. Boats can therefore reach southern Brittany without having to sail around the Finistère point.

Upstream
of the dam
that serves
the tide-power
station, the Rance
offers a succession
of magical
panoramas.
Here, the view
stretches from
Richardais cove
to Landriais cove,
with the islands
of Chevret and
Notre-Dame.
A footpath follows
the left bank of
the estuary, then
the canal, allowing
one to reach
the port of Dinan
on foot; the famous
Montée du Jerzual
then gives access
to the ramparts
and the mediaeval
quarters.

Philip Plisson's images are distributed by Pêcheur d'images Production
and online at www.plisson.com. Contact: philip@plisson.com

Translated from the French by Roland Glasser

Published in 2005 by **Stewart, Tabori & Chang**
All rights reserved.
No part of the contents of this book may be reproduced without the written permission of the copyright holder.
Printed and bound in France by Pollina s.a., - n° L 96200B
10 9 8 7 6 5 4 3 2 1

Stewart, Tabori & Chang is a subsidiary of

ISBN : 1-5847-9442-9